13 Ways to Eat a Fly

Sue Heavenrich

Illustrated by **David Clark**

ini **Charlesbridge**

Big flies,
    small flies,
        fat flies,
            thinner.

Yum! These flies are someone's dinner.

We might think of flies as pests.
But many animals—and plants—
depend on flies for food.

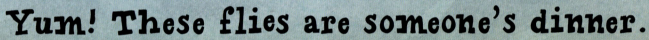

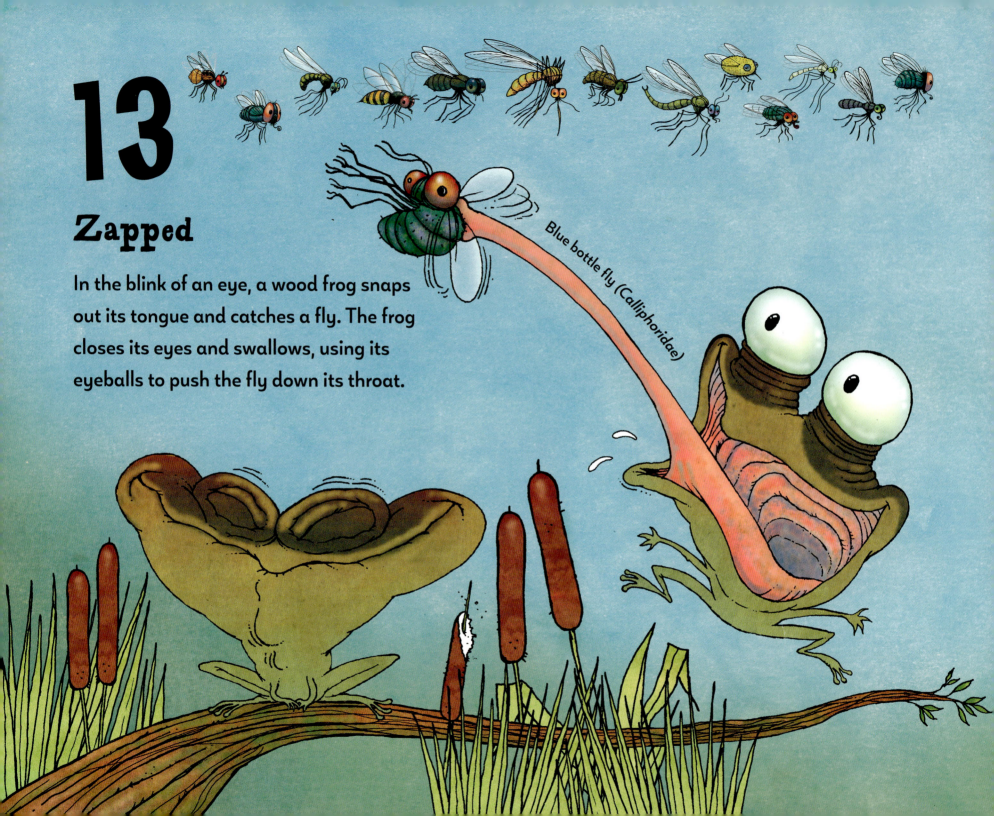

13

Zapped

In the blink of an eye, a wood frog snaps out its tongue and catches a fly. The frog closes its eyes and swallows, using its eyeballs to push the fly down its throat.

Blue bottle fly (Calliphoridae)

12

Wrapped

A fly struggles to escape from sticky threads, sending vibrations along the web. Those vibrations mean dinner to a garden spider. The spider races to the fly and bites it, injecting venom to kill it. Then the spider rolls the fly, wrapping it in silk until it looks like a burrito.

Long-legged fly
(Dolichopodidae)

11

Waterbound

This water strider follows ripples to where a fly is trapped on the surface of the water. The strider grips the fly with its short front legs and stabs it with its beak. If the fly is large enough, the water strider shares its meal with friends.

Crane fly (Tipulidae)

10

Underground

A sand wasp digs a few short tunnels for nests and lays an egg in each one. Once the eggs hatch into larvae, the mama wasp goes hunting. She stings a fly, carries it home, and drags it down into a nest. Then the busy mama heads out on another hunting trip.

Flesh fly (*Sarcophagidae*)

9

Snatched

A well-camouflaged crab spider waits, motionless in a flower. When an unsuspecting fly lands—*pounce!* The spider grabs the fly with its powerful front legs and sinks its fangs into the fly's head.

Bee fly (Bombyliidae)

8

Hatched

Midge (Chironomidae)

When midges hatch, thousands of the tiny, tasty flies cluster above a stream's surface. That's enough to make any trout leap for lunch. *Splash!* One trout can devour five hundred midges in a day.

7

Midflight

Che-BECK! With a flick of its tail, a least flycatcher zooms after its lunch. It snatches a fly in midair and then returns to its perch to finish it off.

Deer fly *(Tabanidae)*

Mosquito (*Culicidae*)

6

Late night

A little brown bat makes high-pitched sounds to find flying insects. When the sounds hit an insect, they bounce back. The echo helps the bat zero in on its prey. With a swoop and a dip, the bat nets the night flier in its tail membrane and then flips it into its mouth.

5

Poked

A sandpiper hunts for spiders and shrimplike crustaceans along a rocky shore. But when the tide comes in, the sandpiper runs to higher ground to munch flies found in rotting kelp.

Kelp fly (*Coelopidae*)

4

Soaked

A six-spotted fishing spider sits on the edge of a leaf with its front feet dangling in the water. Vibrations on the water's surface let the spider know that a fly has fallen in. The spider steps off the leaf, raises its front legs to catch the wind, and glides across the water toward the struggling fly.

Hover fly (*Syrphidae*)

3

Liquefied

An unwary gnat brushes against the sensitive trigger hairs of a Venus flytrap. *Snap!* Bye-bye, fly! Digestive juices inside the leaf dissolve the meaty parts of the fly. In a few days the leaf will open up to let the wind blow away the bits the plant can't digest.

Fungus gnat (Mycetophilidae)

2

Zombified

A fly-eating fungus infects the brain of a fly, turning it into a zombie. The fungus makes the fly climb high—up a plant stem or window screen—while it feeds on the fly's internal organs. When there's nothing left to eat, the fungus oozes out of the fly and shoots spores into the air to infect more flies.

House fly (*Muscidae*)

1

Mediterranean fruit fly
(*Tephritidae*)

By mistake or . . .

If you're sailing down a hill and a fly gets caught
in the back of your throat, don't worry! Aside
from the tickle, swallowing a fly is harmless.

baked in cake

People don't usually eat flies on purpose. But like other insects, flies are high in protein and low in fat. Some people already snack on roasted crickets and spicy grasshoppers, so why not flies? One enterprising team of fly farmers is developing a protein powder made from fruit flies. The powder can be rolled into meatballs, fried into burgers—and even added to cake!

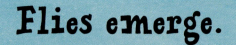

Flies emerge.
Stretch wings and dry.
Tomorrow's lunch
takes to the sky.

You probably won't find flies on your menu anytime soon, but they are a major food source for many birds, fish, mammals, and insects. So next time a fly zooms by, think of it as someone's fast food!

The Non-Human Insectivore's Guide to Fine Dining

If you're going to eat flies, remember: the tastiest flies come from your local area. Look for flies around manure piles and compost bins; in gardens, parks, streams, and ponds; and at the beach. For late-night dining, visit well-lit porches and gas stations.

If you eat out, make sure you're getting what you pay for. Unscrupulous chefs might be tempted to use substitute ingredients, so remember to count the wings. A fly will have only two wings; other insects have four.

Study the menu carefully. There are more than 120,000 kinds of flies, but most establishments serve only a limited variety. Most diners eat flies, wings and all. If, like certain picky spiders, you must remove the wings and legs prior to eating, please dispose of them discreetly.

Nutrition Facts

Serving Size 1g (65–80 flies, depending on species)
Servings Per Container 1

Amount Per Serving

Calories 1

	% of Serving*
Total Fat 0.02	2%
Cholesterol 0 mg	0%
Sodium 0 mg	0%
Total Carbohydrate 0.02 g	2.2%
Dietary Fiber 0.022 g	2.2%
Sugars 0 g	0%
Protein 0.2 g	20%

Vitamins and Minerals		% of Serving*	
Thiamin (B1)	1%	Riboflavin (B2)	7%
Calcium	7%	Iron	1%

Flies are part of a healthy meal. Remember to balance your diet with insects from other food groups.

* Percentage of one-gram serving

Edible parts of a fly

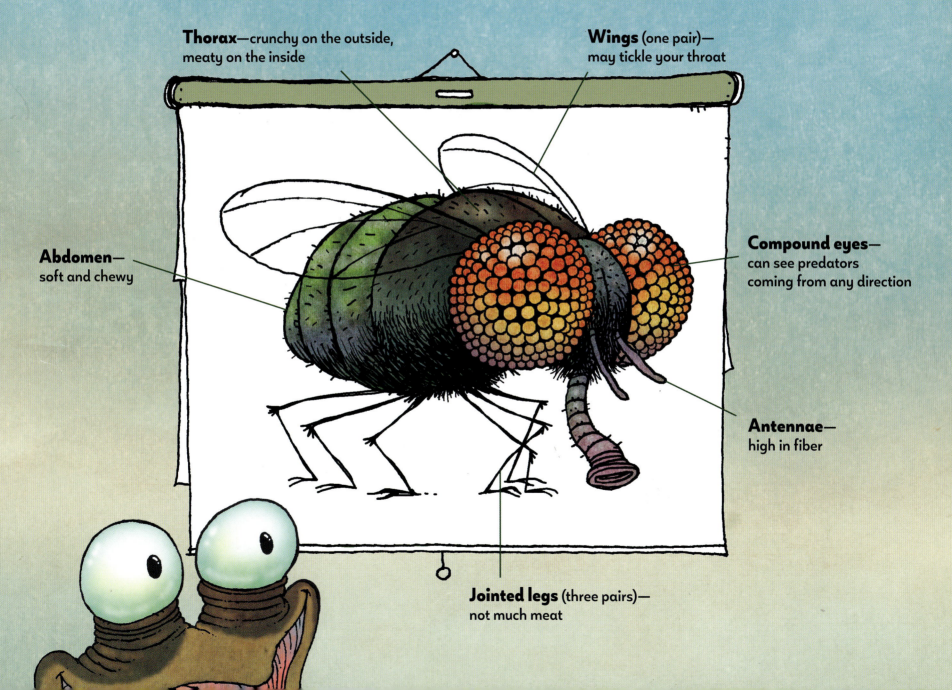

Thorax—crunchy on the outside, meaty on the inside

Wings (one pair)— may tickle your throat

Abdomen— soft and chewy

Compound eyes— can see predators coming from any direction

Antennae— high in fiber

Jointed legs (three pairs)— not much meat

Books

French, Jess. *The Book of Brilliant Bugs.* Illustrated by Claire McElfatrick. London: Dorling Kindersley, 2020.

Gravel, Elise. *The Fly.* Toronto: Tundra Books, 2014.

Heos, Bridget. *I, Fly: The Buzz About Flies and How Awesome They Are.* Illustrated by Jennifer Plecas. New York: Henry Holt, 2015.

Murawski, Darlyne, and Nancy Honovich. *Ultimate Bugopedia: The Most Complete Bug Reference Ever.* Washington, DC: National Geographic Children's Books, 2013.

Spelman, Lucy. *Animal Encyclopedia: 2,500 Animals with Photos, Maps, and More!* Washington, DC: National Geographic Children's Books, 2012.

Websites

"A Tour of the World's Weird and Wonderful Flies." http://www.sciencefriday.com/segments/a-tour-of-the-worlds-weird-and-wonderful-flies/ This Science Friday podcast features Erica McAlister, senior curator at the Natural History Museum in London.

Animal Diversity Web, Diptera https://animaldiversity.org/accounts/Diptera/pictures/ This website by the University of Michigan Museum of Zoology includes photographs and illustrations of flies.

BioKIDS Critter Catalog http://www.biokids.umich.edu/critters/ This website by the University of Michigan contains information about common fly-eating animals found in Michigan and elsewhere.

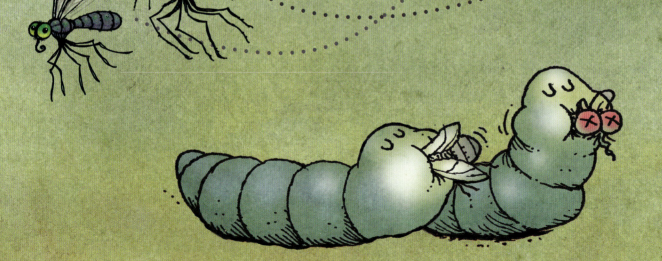

Selected Bibliography

Bat Conservation International. http://www.batcon.org/our-work/.

Borror, Donald J., and Richard E. White. *A Field Guide to Insects: America North of Mexico.* Boston: Houghton Mifflin, 1970.

Evans, Howard Ensign. "Thirteen Ways to Carry a Dead Fly." *Wasp Farm.* Garden City, NY: Published for the American Museum of Natural History by the Natural History Press, 1963.

James, David G. *Beneficial Insects, Spiders, and Other Mini-Creatures in Your Garden: Who They Are and How to Get Them to Stay.* Prosser, WA: Washington State University Extension, 2014. http://pubs.cahnrs.wsu.edu/publications/pubs/em067e.

Martin, Daniella. "List of Edible Insects." Girl Meets Bug. https://edibug.wordpress.com/list-of-edible-insects.

Milne, Lorus Johnson, and Margery Milne. *National Audubon Society Field Guide to North American Insects and Spiders.* New York: A. A. Knopf, 1980.

Myers, P., et al. "Diptera." Animal Diversity Web, University of Michigan. https://animaldiversity.org/accounts/Diptera/classification.

Redmond, Kate. "Bug of the Week." College of Letters & Science Field Station, University of Wisconsin-Milwaukee. http://uwm.edu/field-station/category/bug-of-the-week.

Siciliano, Leon, and Reuters. "An Israeli Food Startup Wants Humans to Eat Fruit Fly Larvae to Save the Planet." *Business Insider.* Oct. 31, 2017. https://www.businessinsider.com/flyingspark-food-startup-wants-humans-to-eat-fruit-fly-larvae-2017-10.

Smithsonian. "True Flies (Diptera)." https://www.si.edu/spotlight/buginfo/true-flies-diptera.

Volk, Thomas J. "Tom Volk's Fungus of the Month for March 2000: This Month's Fungus Is *Entomophthora muscae,* a Fungus That Infects Houseflies." University of Wisconsin-La Crosse. March 2000. http://botit.botany.wisc.edu/toms_fungi/mar2000.html.

A big buzzy thanks to my Narrative Ark
writing partners: Liz, Johanna, Hope,
Jodie, Clara, and Diane—S. H.

To Mary Alice, who would never
harm a fly—D. C.

Text copyright © 2021 by Sue Heavenrich
Illustrations copyright © 2021 by David Clark
All rights reserved, including the right of reproduction in whole
or in part in any form. Charlesbridge and colophon are registered
trademarks of Charlesbridge Publishing, Inc.

At the time of publication, all URLs printed in this book
were accurate and active. Charlesbridge, the author, and the
illustrator are not responsible for the content or accessibility
of any website.

Published by Charlesbridge
9 Galen Street
Watertown, MA 02472
(617) 926-0329
www.charlesbridge.com

Printed in China
(hc) 10 9 8 7 6 5 4 3 2 1

Illustrations done in pen and ink and digital media
Display type set in Handegypt by Matt Desmond, MADType
      and Big Limbo Regular by Bitstream Inc.
Text type set in Blauth by Sofia Mohr
Color separations by Colourscan Print Co Pte Ltd, Singapore
Printed by 1010 Printing International Limited in Huizhou,
      Guangdong, China
Production supervision by Brian G. Walker
Designed by Jon Simeon and Sarah Richards Taylor

Library of Congress Cataloging-in-Publication Data
Names: Heavenrich, Sue, author. | Clark, David, 1960 March 19– illustrator.
Title: 13 ways to eat a fly / Sue Heavenrich ; illustrated by David Clark.
Other titles: Thirteen ways to eat a fly
Description: Watertown, MA : Charlesbridge, [2020] | Summary: "Thirteen
      flies become tasty snacks in this clever reverse counting book about
      predators and prey. Science meets subtraction as a swarm of flies buzzes
      along, losing one member to each predator along the way. Includes a guide
      to eating bugs, complete with nutritional information for a single serving of
      flies."— Provided by publisher.
Identifiers: LCCN 2019014546 (print) | LCCN 2019020247 (ebook) |
      ISBN 9781580898904 (reinforced for library use) |
      ISBN 9781632897541 (ebook)
Subjects: LCSH: Flies—Juvenile literature. | Predation (Biology)—Juvenile
      literature. | Subtraction—Juvenile literature. | Counting—Juvenile literature.
Classification: LCC QL533.2 .H43 2020 (print) | LCC QL533.2 (ebook) |
      DDC 595.77—dc23
LC record available at https://lccn.loc.gov/2019014546
LC ebook record available at https://lccn.loc.gov/2019020247